Python for Beginners

The Crash Course to Learn Programming Python Faster and Remember it Longer. Includes Hands-On Projects and Exercises for Machine Learning, Data Science Analysis, and Artificial Intelligence

Table of Contents

Introduction

Congratulations on downloading Python *for Beginners* and thank you for doing so.

The following chapters will discuss everything that you need to know when it comes to Python coding, and how to use this with data analysis and even machine learning as well. Whether you have worked with other coding languages for a bit, or this is the very first time that you have entered the world of coding, this guidebook has all of the information that you need to get things started with the Python language.

To start this guidebook, we are going to take some time to learn more about the Python language. We will take a look at some of the benefits of the Python code and how you would be able to use this coding language rather than some of the others, how to install Python on the various operating systems that are there, and some of the basic parts of the Python code to help you to get started before we dive into the different parts of this code.

Then we will spend some time to talk about the different options that you can use in order to learn how to do some of your own codings, even as a beginner with Python. Some of the different

types of coding that you are able to do with Python and that we are going to discuss in this guidebook includes how to handle classes and objects, how to create some of your own inheritances, how to create a loop in Python, and working with conditional statements and exception handling.

Once we have some of the basics down and we are able to work with some of these basic coding options that come with Python, it is time to move on to some of the machine learning and data analysis that you are able to do with Python. This part of the guidebook is going to focus on how to create your own data analysis, how to test out the codes that you write, how to handle Python and artificial intelligence, and how machine learning and Python can work together. Then we will end this guidebook with some of the practical codes and exercises that you can do with Python in order to create your own machine learning algorithms as well.

There are a lot of benefits of using Python, especially if you want to be able to get into machine learning, artificial intelligence, and data analysis. All of these can be used with other coding languages if you choose, but Python is the easiest and most efficient to get this done. As a beginner, it may seem like it is impossible to learn how to use these and get ahead, but in this guidebook, we are going to spend time looking at how to do all of this and put it all together to get the results that we want. When you are ready to learn some of the basics that come with Python and how to use it with other options like artificial intelligence and machine learning, make sure to check out this guidebook to learn how to get started.

There are plenty of books on this subject on the market, thanks again for choosing this one! Every effort was made to ensure it is full of as much useful information as possible, please enjoy!

Chapter 1: The Benefits of Working with the Python Language

When it comes to picking out the coding language that you want to work with, there are a lot of different options that you can go with. Some are going to provide you with a lot of power. Some are going to work specifically with certain operating systems. And others are going to work the best when it comes to working on a website or online. But one of the best coding languages for you to work with that will help improve your coding experience and will help you to do a lot of different programming applications, then you have to learn how to work with Python.

Python is going to be a great coding language that helps you to really do a good job with many applications online and for programs that you want to make. It is easy enough for a beginner to use, in fact, it was designed to be used by those who are beginners and who have never coded before, while still having the strength that you need to handle some of the different harder applications, such as machine learning, that you would like to explore.

There are a lot of different benefits that come with using the Python language and this is why so many people like to spend time learning how to work with this kind of language. There are some benefits that you are going to enjoy when you decide to learn how to code with Python.

There are a lot of different support libraries that you are able to use. You will be able to find an extension and a library that works with Python for almost anything that you need. These libraries are great for providing you with the algorithms, the functions, and more that you need in order to get any coding task that you want to be done. You can work with just the traditional library that comes with Python originally, or you can go through and work with some of the other extensions and libraries based on the kind of project you would like to do.

Another benefit that comes with this coding language is all of the different integration features that happen. Python can be a good thing to a programmer because it is going to integrate what is known as the Enterprise Application Integration. This is going to be useful because it can make sure that you can work with different operating systems, different coding languages, and more. There is almost nothing that Python isn't able to help you out with, so learning how to use it can be so great.

Python is also going to provide you with more productivity in the process. The language here is going to be designed as an object-oriented language, and it includes many different kinds of support libraries to help you get things done. Because of these resources, and the ease of use that comes with this language, the programmer is going to be able to get more done in a shorter amount of time. This can even help to improve how much productivity the programmer is going to enjoy while using some different coding languages along with Python.

Many programmers like to go with Python because of the amount of ease of use that comes with it. Python was developed so that it could be as easy to use as possible, and the amount of adaptability that comes with it. This is going to mean that the language is easy to learn, and makes things easier for even a beginner to work with. This guidebook is going to spend some time on the basics, along with some of the things that may seem a bit more complicated, to make sure that you can create some of the projects that you want in this library.

In addition to this language being easy for a beginner to learn, it is also an easy-to-read kind of language. As you go through the different codes that are found with this guidebook, you will be able to read through it, even before you have really learned it too much. There are not a lot of extras that come with it, and you will be able to read through it in no time at all and it won't take long until you can write some of your own codes as well.

Even though it is easier for a lot of beginners to get started with, it is also going to contain a ton of power behind it. Many of those who decide to work with Python is going to be impressed by all of the power that is in this kind of coding language thanks to how easy it is. Even as a beginner language, it is going to contain all of the power that you need to combine with many other languages, and to do almost any kind of application that you want.

The community that comes with this language is also something special that you will love. Python is one of the top languages for programming and coding that are available, which is good news for those who are just getting started. All of the people who are able to use this program can answer your questions, show you different kinds of codes that you can write, and so much more.

And finally, you will enjoy that the Python code is going to be open-sourced. What this means is that you are able to get the basics of Python and a lot of the libraries and extensions that you need with this language for free. There are developers who are working on this language on a constant basis, but you will still be able to use it and download it on your computer for free.

As you can see, there are a lot of benefits that come with working with the Python language, rather than one of the other coding languages that are available. And this is a big reason why so many programmers choose to go with this kind of language over one of the others. Whether it is the first time that you have ever decided to code, or you have been coding for some time, you will find that the Python language is going to be one of the best for you to choose.

Chapter 2: Installing and Working with Python on Different Operating Systems

Now that you have decided to work with the Python code to help you to do some of your own programming and coding, it is time to get to work with installing this on your computer. You will not be able to get all of the work done or use any of the coding languages if all of the different parts and files that come with the Python code are on your computer. This chapter is going to take some time to look at how you can install Python on your computer, no matter which operating system you want to work with.

For these steps, we are going to assume that you are getting Python from www.python.org. There are other resources where you are able to get this programming language, but this one is often the easiest because it is going to have all of the files and extensions that you need to make Python work, and all of them are free to use. Other sources can provide some more features and other things that you need, but they do not always work well or they may be missing some of the parts that you need. So, let's dive in and see how we can get the folders of Python set up with our computer.

Installing on the Mac OS X

The first option that we are going to look at when we want to add on Python to our operating system is the Mac OS X. This is a popular option when it comes to the operating system on a computer, and it is going to work just fine with some of the codings that we decide to do with Python. However, you need to double-check the system because some of Python versions are going to automatically be included on this operating system. To see which version of the Python program is found on your system, it will include the following code:

Python – V

This is going to show you the version you get so a number will come up. You can also choose to install Python 3 on this system if you would like, and it isn't required to uninstall the 2.X version on the computer. To check for the 3.X installation, you just need to open up the terminal app and then type in the following prompt:

Python3 – V

The default on OS X is that Python 3 is not going to be installed at all. If you want to use Python 3, you can install it using some of the installers that are on Python.org. This is a good place to go from because it will install everything that you need to write and execute your codes with Python. It will have the Python shell, the IDLE development tools, and the interpreter. Unlike what happens with Python 2.X, these tools are installed as a standard application in the Applications folder.

Being able to run the IDLE and the Python shell is going to be dependent on which version you choose and some of your own personal preferences. You can use the following commands to help you start the shell and IDLE applications:

- For Python 2.X just type in "Idle"
- For Python 3.X, just type in "Idle3"

Installing on a Windows System

A Windows system is also able to work with Python. There is not going to be a version of this program on Windows though simply because the Windows system has its own programming language that you are able to work with. This does not mean that you are limited to only using that language, but it does mean that you are going to have to spend some time installing Python and picking out the version of Python that you would like to use.

There are a few steps that you are able to use in order to make sure that you can install the Python program on your system. It can look a bit intimidating when you first get started, but you will find that these steps only take a few minutes so it isn't as bad as it seems. Some of the steps that you need to follow in order to make sure that Python is installed properly on your Windows computer will include:

1. To get started with this, it is time to visit the official download page for Python and then grab the Windows Installer. You are able to choose which version of Python that you would like to work with. Your default of this is going to give you the 32-bit version of the language, but you can go through and click on the 64-bit version if this is what you need for your computer system.
2. Now you can go through and push on the right-click button on the installer and then allow it to Run as Administrator. There are going to be a point that gives you two options. You will want to go with the button that allows for customizing the installation.
3. On the following screen, you need to make sure that you look under the part for Optional Features and click on all

of the boxes that are there. When those boxes are filled out, you can click the Next button.

4. While you are still in the part for Advanced Options, you can pick out the location where you would like to install Python. Click on Install and then wait a few minutes in order to get this installation finished. Then close out of the installer when it is all done.

5. At this point, you can set up the PATH variable to the system to make sure that it is going to include all of the directories that come with the packages and to make sure that all of the other components that you need show up as well. The steps that you can follow to make all of this happen includes:

   a. Start this part by opening up your Control Panel. This is easily done by clicking on your taskbar and then typing in "Control Panel". Click on the icon that shows up.

   b. While you are inside this part of the process, it is time to do a search for the Environment. Then you can click on the part that allows you to edit the System Environment Variables. From here, you can then click on the button that allows you to enter into Environment Variables.

   c. Head over to the section that is for User Variables. You can choose to edit the PATH variable that is already there for your use, or you can decide to create a brand new one.

    d. If you see that this system doesn't provide you with a variable for the PATH, then it is time to create your own. You can create this by clicking on NEW. Make the name of the PATH variable and add in the directories that you want. Close all the control Panel dialogs and then click on Next to finish it up.

6. At this point, you are able to open up the command prompt on your Windows computer. This is done by clicking on your Start Menu and then going to the Windows System and then into Command Prompt. Type in the word "python". This will make sure that the interpreter of Python is going to load up for you.

At this point, the program is going to be set up and ready to use on your Windows system. You can choose to open up the other parts of the system as well to make sure that all of the parts that you need are in one place, and then it is time to write out any code that you want when the time is right.

How to install Python on your Linux System

Now that we have been able to explore how to install Python on your Windows computer and your Mac OS X, it is time to move on to some of the steps that you can use to get this language installed on your Linux system as well. There are many individuals and programmers alike who are moving over to the Linux system, so it is one that we need to spend some time learning how to use for our needs.

The first thing to do here is to see if there is a version of Python 3 already on your system. You can open up the command prompt on Linux and then run the following code:

```
$ python3 - - version
```

If you are on Ubuntu 16.10 or newer, then it is a simple process to install Python 3.6. You just need to use the following commands:

```
$ sudo apt-get update
$ sudo apt-get install Python3.6
```

If you are relying on an older version of Ubuntu or another version, then you may want to work with the deadsnakes PPA, or another tool, to help you download the Python 3.6 version. The code that you need to do this includes:

```
$ sudo apt-get install software-properties-common
```

```
$ sudo add-apt repository ppa:deadsnakes/ppa
# suoda apt-get update
$ sudo apt-get install python3.6
```

The thing to remember here is that if you have spent some time working with a few of the other distributions that come with Linux, it is likely that your system is going to have a version of Python 3 already installed on there. If you do not see this here, you can choose to use the package manager of the distribution. Or you can go through the steps that we have above in order to help you to install any version of Python that you want before using the program.

Understanding the Interpreter in Python

The standard installation of Python, when you do it on python.org, is going to contain documentation, information on licensing, and three main files to execute that help you develop and then run the scripts that you run on python. These include the Python interpreter, IDLE, and Shell.

First is the Python interpreter. This is important because it is responsible for executing the scripts that you decide to write. The interpreter can convert the .py script files into instructions and then processes them according to the type of code that you write in the file.

Then there is the Python IDLE. This is known as the integrated development and learning environment. It is going to contain all of the tools that are needed to develop your programs in Python. You will find tools for debugging, the text editor, and the shell with this. Depending on the version of Python that you choose, the IDLE can either be extensive or pretty basic. You can also pick out your own IDLE if there is another version that you like better. Many people like to find new text editors because they think the one with Python doesn't have the right features, but the one from Python is just fine for the codes we will do so it's not necessary to pick a different one.

Then there is the Python Shell. This is an interactive command line-driven interface that is found in the interpreter. This is going to hold onto the commands that you decide to write out. If the shell understands what you are writing, then it will go through and execute the code that you write. But if it doesn't understand the code, or you write it out incorrectly, then it will return an error message to you.

All of these can be important when it comes to writing out your code. When working with the installation through python.org, they will be installed for you and you won't need to go through and do any other work to make it happen. If you get the Python version from some other location, check the files that you get and see if you need to make some changes or add these onto your computer to write your code.

Chapter 3: Some of the Basic Parts of the Python Code

Now that we have learned a bit more about the Python code, and some of the things that you need to do in order to get this coding language set up on your computer, it is time to take a look at some of the different things that you can do with your code. We are going to start out with some of the basics, and then will build on this when we get a bit further on in this guidebook to see some of the other things that we are able to do with this language. With this in mind, let's take a look at some of the basics that you need to know about any code in Python, and all that you are going to be able to do with this coding language.

The Keywords in Python

The first part of the Python code that we are going to focus on is the Python keywords. These keywords are going to be reserved because they give the commands over to the compiler. You do not want to let these keywords show up in other parts of the code, and it is important to know that you are using them in the right part of the code.

Any time that you are using these keywords in the wrong manner, or in the wrong part of the code, you are going to end up with some errors in place. These keywords are going to be there to tell your compiler what you wanted to happen, allowing it to know what it should do at the different parts of the code. They are really important to the code and will make sure that everything works the proper manner and at the right times.

How To Name The Identifiers in your Code

The next thing that we need to focus on for a moment when it comes to your code is working with the identifiers. There are a lot of different identifiers that you are able to work with, and they do come in a variety of names including classes, variables, entities, and functions. The neat thing that happens when you go through the process of naming an identifier is that the same rules are going to apply no matter what name you have, which can make it easier for a beginner to remember the different rules that come with them.

So, let's dive into some of the rules that we need to remember when doing these identifiers. You have a lot of different options to keep in mind when you decide to name the identifiers. For example, you can rely on using all kinds of letters, whether they are lowercase or uppercase. Numbers work well, too. You will be allowed to bring in the underscore symbol any time that you would like. And any combination of these together can help you to finish up the naming that you want to do.

One thing to remember with the naming rules though is that you should not start the name with any kind of number, and you do not want to allow any kind of space between the words that you are writing out. So, you would not want to pick out the name of 5kids, but you could call it fivekids. And five kids for a name would not work, but five_kids would be fine.

When you are working on the name for any of the identifiers that you want to create in this kind of coding language, you need to make sure that you are following the rules above, but add to this that the name you choose has to be one that you are able to remember later. You are going to need to, at some point, pull that name back up, and if you picked out one that is difficult to remember or doesn't make sense in the code that you are doing, and you can't call it back up, it is going to raise an error or another problem along the way. Outside of these rules, you will be fine naming the identifier anything that makes sense for that part of the code.

How to Handle the Control Flow with Python

The control flow in this language can be important. This control flow is there to ensure that you wrote out the code the proper way. There are some types of strings in your code that you may want to write out so that the compiler can read them the right way. But if you write out the string in the wrong manner, you are going to end up with errors in the system. We will take a look at many codes into this guidebook that follows the right control flow for this language, which can make it easier to know what you need to get done and how you can write out codes in this language.

The Python Statements

The next topic that we need to take a look at when we do some of our codings is the idea of the statements. These are going to be a simple thing to work on when it comes to Python. They are simply going to be strings of code that you are able to write out, and then you will tell the compiler to show that string on the computer string at the right time.

When you give the compiler the instructions that it needs to follow, you will find that there are going to be statements that come with it. As long as you write these statements out in the right manner, the compiler is going to be able to read them and will show the message that you have chosen on the computer screen. You are able to choose to write these statements out as long or as short as you would like, and it all is going to depend on the kind of code that you are trying to work on at the time.

The Importance of the Python Comments

Any time that you are writing out new code in Python, it is important to know how to work with the comments. You may find that as you are working on the various parts of your code, and changing things around, you may want to add a note or name a part of the code or leave any other explanation that helps to know what that part of the code is all about. These notes are things that you and anyone else who is reading through the code will be able to see and utilize, but they are not going to affect the code. The compiler knows that comment is going on, and will just skip that and go to the next part of the code that you wrote out.

Making your own comment in Python is a pretty easy process. You just need to add in the # symbol before the note that you want to write, and then the compiler knows that a note is there and that it doesn't need to read that part of the code at all. It is possible for you to go through and add in as many of these comments to the code that you are writing as you would like and you could fill up the whole code with comments. The compiler would be able to handle this but the best coding practice is to just add in the amount that you really need. This helps to keep things organized and ensures that you are going to have things looking nice and neat.

Variables in Python

Variables are another part of the code that you will need to know about because they are so common in your code. The variables are there to help store some of the values that you place in the code, helping them to stay organized and nice. You can easily add in some of the values to the right variable simply by using the equal sign. It is even possible for you to take two values and add them to the same variables if you want and you will see this occur in a few of the codes that we discuss through this guidebook. Variables are very common and you will easily see them throughout the examples that we show.

Looking for the Operators

Another part of the code that we can focus on when working in the Python language is the idea of the operators. These are simple to use, and there are going to be a lot of the codes that you try to work on that will include these operators. But even though they are pretty easy to work with, they can add to a level of power that is so important to a lot of the codes that you want. And there are a variety of operators that you are able to focus on when you write a Python code so you have some options.

For example, you can start out with the arithmetic functions. These are good ones to work with any time that you need to do some kind of mathematics with your code. There are going to be the assignment operators that make sure a value is assigned over to the variable that you are working on. There can be comparison operators as well which allow you to take two parts of the code, or the code and the input from the user, and then compare them to see if they are the same or not and then reacting in the way that you would like based on the code that you wrote.

As you can see, there are a ton of different parts that come with the basics of the Python code. Many of these are going to be seen in the types of codes that you are trying to write out in Python, and can really help you to start writing out some of your own codes. As we go through some of the examples, as well as the practice exercises, as we go through this guidebook, you will find that these basics are going to be found in a lot of the codes that you would like to work on.

Chapter 4: How to Work Classes and Objects

One of the things that you will really enjoy working on when it comes to Python is the organization that comes with it. This kind of coding language is going to spend time dividing everything up into classes and objects. This allows for more organization, ensures that every part of the code has a place and won't get lost, and really makes it easier for the beginner programmer to get things done without as much hassle.

Before we go through and create a new class, it is time to look a bit closer at what these classes and objects are all about. The objects are going to be anything that you are able to find in the real world. You will have a lot of objects that can work in the Python language, and these are going to help to power the code that you are working with, and will ensure that your code behaves in the manner that you would like. You can have any kind of object that you want, and they would match one of the objects that you want to do in the real world.

And then we have the classes. The best way to think about the classes in our Python code is as a little box that holds onto those objects that you created before. This helps to provide us with some organization when it comes to the code because we can place all of the objects that we want into each class, and then easily pull them back out at a later time when we want.

You can make as many classes as you would like in the code, and you get the benefit of being able to add in any objects, and as many objects, as you would like into each class. The biggest thing to remember here is that you need to make sure that the objects that belong to each class go together and make sense together. If someone else came in and looked at the coding that you did, and looked into one of the classes, would they be able to tell why all of those objects were found in the same class?

This doesn't mean that all of the objects in one class has to be exactly the same. But they need to make sense out of it as much as possible. You do not have to have a class that is just cars, for example, unless you would like to have it this way. But you could also go with a class that is going to contain different vehicles and this would be just fine as well.

How to Create a Class

With the information behind us about what these classes and objects are all about, it is time for us to take a look at the steps that we need to follow in order to create one of our own classes along the way. It is important to learn how to create our own classes because it is going to make sure that we have everything in place and we won't lose anything at the same time.

To make sure that you get the class ready to go, you need to put the right kind of keyword in place and then go through and name the class. You get the freedom here to give the class any name that you would like, but it is important to come up with a name that makes sense, and you have to place the name after the keyword so that the compiler knows what is going on.

After naming the class, it is time to name a subclass, which will be placed inside parenthesis to stick with proper programming rules. Make sure that at the end of that first line, whenever you create a class, that you add in a semicolon. While this isn't technically needed with most newer versions of Python and the code is going to work even if you forget this part, it is still considered part of coding etiquette to do this so make sure that you put it in.

Writing a class sounds more complicated than it really is, so let's stop here and look at an example of how you would write this out in Python. Then we can discuss what the parts mean and why they are important. A good example of creating a class with Python includes the following:

```python
class Vehicle(object):
#constructor
def_init_(self, steering, wheels, clutch, breaks, gears):
self._steering = steering
self._wheels = wheels
self._clutch = clutch
self._breaks =breaks
self._gears  = gears
#destructor
def_del_(self):
    print("This is destructor....")


#member functions or methods
def Display_Vehicle(self):
   print('Steering:' , self._steering)
   print('Wheels:', self._wheels)
   print('Clutch:', self._clutch)
   print('Breaks:', self._breaks)
   print('Gears:', self._gears)
#instantiate a vehicle option
myGenericVehicle = Vehicle('Power Steering', 4, 'Super Clutch',
'Disk Breaks', 5)

myGenericVehicle.Display_Vehicle()
```

To see how this is going to work well for your needs and how the class can be set up, you should open up your compiler and type in the code that we have above. This will ensure that you are going to be able to test out the code and see which kind of class you have been able to create. This is a simple code that ensures we have the right objects that go into the different class that we assigned, and will make sure that when we open up that class, it is all going to open up and work the way that we would like.

How to access some of the members of our class

As you look at the code that we wrote above, you can see that we took some time to go through and create a class and then added in a few objects to this as well. This is going to make it so that our objects are in the same place and can make it easier to pull them all out and make them easier to use in the long run. But now that the class is done, it is time to look at some of the objects that we put into that class and then learn how to pull them out.

In this part of the code, we have to learn the steps that are needed to access members of that class that we were able to create above. You want to make sure that your text editor and your compiler will be able to recognize all of the classes that you design later on because this is going to ensure that both of those are able to execute the code in the right manner.

Now, to set up the code that you want to right, you need to make sure that you set it up right, and there are a few methods that work for this. We are going to look at the accessor method to get this done because it is the easiest in most cases, and it is the one that most programmers are going to work with as well. To understand how you would use the method of the accessor function, look at the code below to help you get started:

```
class Cat(object)
        itsAge = None
        itsWeight = None
        itsName = None
        #set accessor function use to assign values to the fields
or member vars
        def setItsAge(self, itsAge):
        self.itsAge = itsAge

        def setItsWeight(self, itsWeight):
        self.itsWeight = itsWeight

        def setItsName(self, itsName):
        self.itsName =itsName
```

#get accessor function use to return the values from a
field
    def getItsAge(self):
    return self.itsAge
    def getItsWeight(self):
    return self.itsWeight

    def getItsName(self):
    return self.itsName

objFrisky = Cat()
objFrisky.setItsAge(5)
objFrisky.setItsWeight(10)
objFrisky.setItsName("Frisky")
print("Cats Name is:", objFrisky.getItsname())
print("Its age is:", objFrisky.getItsAge())
print("Its weight is:", objFrisky.getItsName())

Classes are not meant to be difficult to work with. They are perfect for helping you to take care of your information and keep it in order so that it makes the most sense. You can create any kind of class that you would like and fill it up with any objects that you like, as long as those objects match each other in some way. Both the objects and classes are going to make a difference in your code to keep it organized, easy to read, and working properly.

Chapter 5: Creating your Own Inheritance

The next topic of coding in Python that we are going to take a look at is known as the inheritance. This is going to seem a bit complicated in the beginning, but it is a great way for you to work on developing some of your coding skills, and will make it easier for you to reuse parts of your code and save some of the coding and the mess that can come from rewriting out all of the different parts that you usually would.

Working with these inheritances is a good way to make sure that your code gets the enhancements that you want inside of Python. These inheritances are going to save us time and can make sure that the ending coding that we want is nicer looking and cleaner in the long run. These inheritances are going to help you to take some of the code that you wrote out earlier and reuse them without having to spend so much time rewriting them out over and over again. Remember that these are going to be unique to Python and other OOP languages, and can be one of the perks of this kind of language.

To keep things as simple as possible, when you are working with the inheritance, you are going to work with the parent code, which is the original code that you want to copy, and then move it down into the new part of the code, making changes to the parts that you want, and then reusing the parts that you like. You can use this to help move the code forward without rewriting it, or just to make the code stronger in some cases. Even as a beginner, it is possible to use these inheritances to help you reuse the code as much as you need to, without having to waste time and room rewriting it out each time.

During the process of working with an inheritance, you would make sure that you take the parent code and then get it all copied over to some other part of the program that you need. The new part that you create is going to be the child code, and it is unique because you can pick and choose which parts of the parent code you would like to keep and which parts you are going to throw out. you can go through this process as many times as you would like to get the code to behave properly.

To help make more sense out of these inheritances, how they work, and how they can help to keep your code clean and tidy and save you time, let's take a look at an example of how they look in your code:

#Example of inheritance
#base class

```python
class Student(object):
        def __init__(self, name, rollno):
        self.name = name
        self.rollno = rollno
#Graduate class inherits or derived from Student class
class GraduateStudent(Student):
        def __init__(self, name, rollno, graduate):
        Student __init__(self, name, rollno)
        self.graduate = graduate

def DisplayGraduateStudent(self):
        print"Student Name:", self.name)
        print("Student Rollno:", self.rollno)
        print("Study Group:", self.graduate)

#Post Graduate class inherits from Student class
class PostGraduate(Student):
        def __init__(self, name, rollno, postgrad):
        Student __init__(self, name, rollno)
        self.postgrad = postgrad

    def DisplayPostGraduateStudent(self):
    print("Student Name:", self.name)
    print("Student Rollno:", self.rollno)
    print("Study Group:", self.postgrad)
```

#instantiate from Graduate and PostGraduate classes

    objGradStudent = GraduateStudent("Mainu", 1, "MS-Mathematics")

    objPostGradStudent = PostGraduate("Shainu", 2, "MS-CS")

    objPostGradStudent.DisplayPostGraduateStudent()

When you type this into your interpreter, you are going to get the results:

('Student Name:', 'Mainu')

('Student Rollno:', 1)

('Student Group:', 'MSC-Mathematics')

('Student Name:', 'Shainu')

('Student Rollno:', 2)

('Student Group:', 'MSC-CS')

You are able to go through this process and use the base or parent class as many times as you would like. It is easy to go down the line as many times as your code asks for, making changes along the way without worrying about ruining up any of the parent code along the way. As long as you do not work on a circular inheritance here, you will be fine to keep adding in the base classes down to the child class, and you will be able to get things to change and stay the same as much as you want as well.

Inheritances can be nice because they allow you to keep using a part of the code that you already created in order to create new parts of your code. This can keep the program code looking nice and saves you a lot of time in the process. Learning how to work with these inheritances will help you to really enhance your codes, keeps it all set up and clean, and will ensure that your codes will work the way that you want.

Chapter 6: Creating a Loop in Python

Loops are going to be next on the list of topics we need to explore when we are working with Python. These are going to be a great way to clean up some of the code that you are working on so that you can add in a ton of information and processing in the code, without having to go through the process of writing out all those lines of code. For example, if you would like a program that would count out all of the numbers that go from one to one hundred, you would not want to write out that many lines of code along the way. Or if you would like to create a program for doing a multiplication table, this would take forever as well. But doing a loop can help to get all of this done in just a few lines of code, saving you a lot of time and code writing in the process.

It is possible to add in a lot of different information into the loops that you would like to write, but even with all of this information, they are still going to be easy to work with. These loops are going to have all of the ability to tell your compiler that it needs to read through the same line of code, over and over again, until the program has reached the conditions that you set. This helps to simplify the code that you are working on while still ensuring that it works the way that you want when executing it.

As you decide to write out some of these loops, it is important to remember to set up the kind of condition that you would like to have met before you ever try to run the program. If you just write out one of these loops, without this condition, the loop won't have any idea when it is time to stop and will keep going on and on. Without this kind of condition, the code is going to keep reading through the loop and will freeze your computer. So, before you execute this code, double-check that you have been able to put in these conditions before you try to run it at all.

As you go through and work on these loops and you are creating your own Python code, there are going to be a few options that you can use with loops. There are a lot of options but we are going to spend our time looking at the three main loops that most programmers are going to use, the ones that are the easiest and most efficient.

The while loop

Out of the three loops that we are going to discuss in this guidebook, we are going to start out with the while loop. The while loop is going to be one that will tell the compiler the specific times that you would like it to go through with that loop. This could be a good loop to use any time that you want the compiler to count from one to ten. With this example, your condition would tell the compiler to stop when it reaches ten, so that it doesn't freeze and keep going. This is also a good option that programmers like to work with because it will make sure that it goes through the code at least one time, if not more before it decides to head on to the other parts of the code that you are writing. To see a good example of how you can work with the while loop take a look at the code that we have below for reference:

#calculation of simple interest. Ask the user to input the principal, rate of interest, number of years.

```
counter = 1
while(counter <= 3):
        principal = int(input("Enter the principal amount:"))
        numberofyeras = int(input("Enter the number of
years:"))
        rateofinterest = float(input("Enter the rate of interest:"))
        simpleinterest = principal * numberofyears *
rateofinterest/100
        print("Simple interest = %.2f" %simpleinterest)
        #increase the counter by 1
```

```
counter = counter + 1
print("You have calculated simple interest for 3 time!")
```

This example allows your user to go through and place the information that pertains to them inside the program. The code will them computer the interest rates based on the information that the user provides. For this one, we set up the while (right at the beginning of the code) and told it to only go through the loop three times. You can change it to go through the process as many times as you would like.

The for loop

Now that we have had some time to look at the while loop, it is time to take a look at what is known as the for loop and how we are able to use this in some of the codings that we want to do. When you would like to bring out the for loop there are going to be some differences compared to the while loop from before. Keep in mind here that most programmers are going to consider the for loop the traditional form of coding. You can use this one in many of the situations where you would work with the while loop so it is important to learn how to use this for your needs.

When you are ready to create your own for loop, the user is not going to be the one who would go through here and provide the code with information that is needed to start the loop. Rather than having this happen, the for loop is set up to go through an iteration in whatever order you put it into the code. There is no need to have this kind of input from the user because the loop is set up to just go through the full iteration until it reaches the end. To see how the for loop works, and how it is going to be different from the while loop that we talked about above, take a look at the code below:

```
# Measure some strings:
words = ['apple', 'mango', 'banana', 'orange']
for w in words:
print(w, len(w))
```

Write this code into your compiler and then execute it. The for loop is going to make sure that all the words in the line above it are shown up on the screen, exactly how you wrote them out. If you want them in a different order, you need to do that as you work on the code, not later on. You can add in any words or other information that you want to show up in this kind of loop, just make sure that you have it in the right order from the beginning.

The nested loop

And the third type of loop that we are going to take a look at is known as the nested loop. If you are working on a code that needs a nested loop, you will take either the for loop or the while loop and you will take that one and place it into another loop. In the code, both of these are going to end up running at the same time, and it is going to continue on in this manner until both of these codes are all the way done.

There are a lot of situations where the nested loop is going to be useful and you will want to add it into your code to get things done. A good example of how this is going to work is when you would like to create a multiplication table. The code that can be useful to help you to make your own multiplication table in the Python language with the help of the nested loop would be the following:

 # write a multiplication table from 1 to 10
For x in xrange(1, 11):
*   For y in xrange(1, 11):*
*   Print '%d = %d' % (x, y, x*x)*

When you got the output of this program, it is going to look similar to this:

1*1 = 1

1*2 = 2

1*3 = 3

1*4 = 4

All the way up to 1*10 = 2

Then it would move on to do the table by twos such as this:

2*1 =2

2*2 = 4

And so on until you end up with 10*10 = 100 as your final spot in the sequence

Any time you need to get one loop to run inside another loop, the nested loop will be able to help you get this done. You can combine together the for loop, the while loop, or each combination based on what you want to get done inside the code. But it definitely shows you how much time and space inside the code that these loops can save. The multiplication table above only took up four lines to write out and you got a huge table. Think of how long this would take if you had to write out each part of the table!

The for loop, the while loop, and the nested loop are the most common types of loops that beginners will use when writing their own codes in Python. You can use these codes to get a lot of work done in your chosen program without having to write out as many lines. You can use it to make sure that a certain part of your code will go through and rewrite itself.

Chapter 7: Working with the Conditional Statements

There are going to be times when you will work on a program in Python where you will need the program to make some decisions for you, without you being there to tell it how to answer each response that it gets. You can set up the conditions that need to be met to help out with this but there is a lot of unknown when the user is allowed to add in any input that they want, and the conditional statements are going to help you learn how to do this. Since you are not able to handle or guess all of the answers or inputs that the user may give, and so these conditional statements are going to be there to help you get things done.

You will find that these conditional statements are going to be a bit different than what you are used to, but they can work on a lot of different programs that you try to write. They are simple, but it is easy to add to them and change things up so that you are able to get more done, and you can handle any of the answers that your users decide to use

When it comes to working with these conditional statements, there are going to be three options that you are able to work with. These are the if statement, the elif statement, and the if else statement. These are all important, but they are going to work in slightly different ways in order to help you to get some of the codings that you want to be done. Let's explore how each of these is going to work inside your own code.

Starting with the if statement

Out of the conditional statements, the most basic of the three and the one that we are going to focus on first is going to be the if statement. The if statement is a basic conditional statement, and sometimes is going to seem too simple to use on a regular basis. In fact, it is more common that you are going to work with the if else statement or the elif statement when in this kind of field, but it is still important to learn how to work with the if statement so that we get some of the basics that come with this kind of conditional statement:

You can probably already guess that this will cause some problems with most codes, but it is still important to know how to use these statements. A simple code that you can work with for these conditional statements include:

age = int(input("Enter your age:"))
if (age <=18):

print("You are not eligible for voting, try next election!")
print("Program ends")

There are a few things that will show up with this code. If you have a user go to the program and state that their age is under 18, then the program will work and display the message that is listed there. The user can read this message and then end the program right there.

Now one thing to notice here is that there is a chance for things to not go as planned when you are working with this kind of code. If the user wants to put in an answer for their age that is 18 or higher, then the code is not set up at this point to handle this issue. Right now, the program is going to only list out the message that you have when the user puts their age in as something under 18. But if they wrote out their age as something higher, then it is not going to meet up with the conditions that you have, and nothing will happen.

Of course, we do not want to have a code where only one answer is right, at least now when it comes to the age of the person using the program. They want to be able to put in their real age at the time, and this may or may not be below 18. You want to make sure that your program is working the way that you want, and this is why we will move on to the if else statements.

Moving on to the if else statements

While the if statements are a good place to get some practice when it comes to writing your own codes in Python, there are not going to be a ton of times in programming when you would want to use these at all. It is likely that you don't want to leave the screen empty with nothing there for the user to see. And this is why we want to learn how to work with the if else statement to handle the issues from above.

The if else statement is going to take the things that we have looked at in the if statement, but moves them along another step so they make more sense and can handle more situations. With the example that we had worked on before, the user is going to be able to see the message we had before if they put in any age under 18. But then this goes a bit further because it is also going to provide us with a message if the user is older than 18 as well. This if else statement is going to make sure that the user is going to get some kind of message, no matter what age they put into the system at the time.

With the voting example that we had above, you can implement the following code to make an if else statement:

```
age = int(input("Enter your age:"))
if (age <=18):
        print("You are not eligible for voting, try next election!")
else
        print("Congratulations! You are eligible to vote. Check
out your local polling station to find out more information!)
print("Program ends")
```

With this option, you are adding in the else statement, which will cover every age that doesn't fall under 18. This way, if the user does list that as their age, something will still pull up on the screen for them. This can provide you with more freedom when working on your code and you can even add in a few more layers to this. If you want to divide it up so that you get four or five age groups and each one gets a different response, you simply need to add in more if statements to make it happen. The else statement is at the end to catch everything else.

We can take this a bit further to see how things go. Let's say that we want to create a code using the if else statement in order to ask our users what their favorite color is. You would continue on with the if statements based on the colors you would like to choose. You are not able to list out all of the colors that are available because this would take forever and be hard to work on but maybe you choose five colors and give them if statements with a message that is attached.

Then, if the user doesn't pick one of those five colors that you put an if statement with, it will be caught by the else statement as well. This ensures that all answers are caught and responded to, without having to worry about listing out and guessing all of the different possibilities that the user can put in.

Finishing it out with the elif statements

Now that we have had some time to explore a bit with the if statement and the if else statement, it is time to take a look at how the elif statement is going to be the same or different, and how you can use it in your code. You will find that these add in a different kind of level to the codes that you are writing, but they still have ease of use to them.

It is possible to write in as many of the elif statements as you would like to the code, and then you also need to add in the else statement, as we did above with the if else statement, to cover any of the other decisions that need to be handled in the code. You can think of the elif statement like something similar to some of the older games out there, the ones that had a menu of options and allowed the user to pick from one of these. This is pretty similar to how we are going to set up our elif statements.

When you are working on these elif statements, you are able to add in as many different options as you would like to finish it up. Sometimes, you may just add one, two, or three, but you are not limited by this and can add in as many as you would like. Keep in mind though that the more elif statements that you add into the code, the messier it gets and the more that you have to write out. To see how the coding for the elif statements is going to work, make sure to check out the following code:

```
Print("Let's enjoy a Pizza! Ok, let's go inside Pizzahut!")
print("Waiter, Please select Pizza of your choice from the
menu")
pizzachoice = int(input("Please enter your choice of Pizza:"))
if pizzachoice == 1:
        print('I want to enjoy a pizza napoletana')
elif pizzachoice == 2:
        print('I want to enjoy a pizza rustica')
elif pizzachoice == 3:
        print('I want to enjoy a pizza capricciosa')
else:
        print("Sorry, I do not want any of the listed pizza's,
please bring a Coca Cola for me.")
```

With this option, the user is able to choose the type of pizza they want to enjoy, but you can use the same syntax for anything you need in your code. If the user pushes the number 2 in the code, they are going to get a pizza Rustica. If they don't like any of the options, then they are telling the program that they just want to have something to drink, in this case, a Coca Cola.

This is a simple way to use elif statements to give the user a set of choices. In the other options, the user could add in any choice that they wanted, but in the elif statement, they can either pick that they want one of the choices that you provide, or they will have to go with the default option at the end. This can work well for many games that you may want to pick, for some tests online, and other programs where you want to limit the choices that the user gets to pick from in the code.

As you can see, there are a lot of different things that you are able to do when working on these conditional statements. You are able to choose what conditions you would like to have in place, and then make sure that the program is going to behave in the right way the whole time. You can choose whether the if statement, the if else statement or the elif statement is going to be the right one for you, and then add these to the code that you are writing.

Chapter 8: Exception Handling in the Python Language

The next topic that we need to spend some time exploring in this guidebook is the idea of exception handling. There are going to be times when your code tries to show up some errors or other problem inside the code that you are doing, and this is where the exception is going to occur. Knowing when to recognize these exceptions, how to handle them, and even how to make some of your own can make a big difference in how well you are able to do some of your own coding in Python.

These exceptions are going to be brought up by the compiler in a lot of different situations, and sometimes, they are going to look like a simple error message like you may have seen on your own computer before. It is important to really read through any of these exceptions that come up in your code and read through them so that you can learn what they are about, and how you can handle them properly at the same time. This isn't meant to be something to scare you, but there are things that you can do to handle these exceptions and to make sure that you are going to be able to handle them in the proper manner.

Now, there are going to be a few exceptions that are already recognized inside the library that you are using in Python. If you want to write out a code with them in there, or if you find that the user is trying to do something that isn't proper for your program, then the compiler is going to send out an exception about this in order to get it to stop. In some cases, the program you are writing is going to need some extra limitations in place to handle it, and you can raise up, after creating, your own exception.

A good example of an exception that your compiler is automatically going to raise up is when you or the user is to divide it by zero. The compiler is then going to recognize that this is something the user is not able to do, and it is going to send out that exception as an alert. It can also be something that is going to be called up if you, as the programmer, are trying to call up a function and the name is not spelled in the proper manner so there is no match present to bring up.

There are a few different exceptions that are automatically found in your Python library. It is a good idea to take some time to look through them and recognize these exceptions so you can recognize them later on. Some of the most common exceptions that you need to worry about include:

- Finally—this is the action that you will want to use to perform cleanup actions, whether the exceptions occur or not.
- Assert—this condition is going to trigger the exception inside of the code
- Raise—the raise command is going to trigger an exception manually inside of the code.
- Try/except—this is when you want to try out a block of code and then it is recovered thanks to the exceptions that either you or the Python code raised.

Raising an Exception

The first thing that we need to take a look at, now that we know a bit more about these exceptions and what they mean, is how to write one out, and some of the steps that you can use if one of these does end up in your own code. If you are going through some of the code writing, and you start to notice that an exception will be raised, know that often the solution is going to be a simple one. But as the programmer, you need to take the time to get this fixed. To help us get started here, let's take a look at what the syntax of the code for raising an exception is all about.

x = 10

```
y = 10
result = x/y #trying to divide by zero
print(result)
```

The output that you are going to get when you try to get the interpreter to go through this code would be:

```
>>>
Traceback (most recent call last):
    File "D: \Python34\tt.py", line 3, in <module>
    result = x/y
ZeroDivisionError: division by zero
>>>
```

As we take a moment to look at the example that we have here, we can see that the program is going to bring up an exception for us, mainly because we are trying to divide a number by zero and this is something that is not allowed in the Python code (and any other coding language for that matter). If you decide not to make any changes at this point, and you go ahead and run the program as it is, you could end up with the compiler sending you an error message. The code is going to tell the user the problem, but as you can see, the problem is not listed out in an easy-to-understand method and it is likely the user will have no idea what is going on or how they can fix the problem at all.

With that example that we worked on above, you have some options. You can choose to leave the message that is kind of confusing if you don't know any coding, or you can add in a new message that is easier to read and explains why this error has been raised in the first place. It won't have a lot of numbers and random letters that only make sense to someone who has done coding for a bit, which makes the whole thing a bit more user-friendly overall. The syntax that you can use to control the message that your user is going to see includes:

```
x = 10
y = 0
result = 0
try:
        result = x/y
        print(result)
except ZeroDivisionError:
        print("You are trying to divide by zero.")
```

Take a look at the two codes above. The one that we just did looks a little bit similar to the one above it, but this one has a message inside. This message is going to show up when the user raises this particular exception. You won't get the string of letters and numbers that don't make sense, and with this one, the user will know exactly what has gone wrong and can fix that error.

Can I define my own exceptions?

In the examples above, we took some time to define and handle the exceptions that the compiler offered to us and are already found in the Python library. Now it is time for us to take it a bit further and learn how to raise a few of our own exceptions in any kind of code that we want to write. Maybe you are working on a code that only allows for a few choices to the user, one that only allows them to pick certain numbers or one that only allows them to have so many chances at guessing. These are common things that we see when we work with gaming programs but can work well in other programs that you design.

When you make these kinds of exceptions, the compiler is going to have to be told that an exception is being raised, because it is not going to see that there is anything wrong in this part of the code. The programmer has to go in and let the compiler know what rules it has to follow, and what exceptions need to be raised in the process. A good example of the syntax that you can use to make this happen in your own code will be below:

class CustomException(Exception):

```
def_init_(self, value):
        self.parameter = value
def_str_(self):
        return repr(self.parameter)


try:
        raise CustomException("This is a CustomError!")
except CustomException as ex:
        print("Caught:", ex.parameter)
```

In this code, you have been successful in setting up your own exceptions and whenever the user raises one of these exceptions, the message of "Caught: This is a CustomError!" is going to come up on the screen. This is the best way to show your users that you have added in a customer exception into the program, especially if this is just one that you personally created for this part of the code, and not one that the compiler is going to recognize on its own.

Just like with the other examples that we went through, we worked with some generic wording just to show how exceptions are able to work. You can easily go through and change this up so that you get a message that is unique for the code that you are writing and will explain to the user what is going on when they get the error message to show up.

Learning how to work with some of the exceptions that can come up in your code is one of the best ways to make sure that your codes work the way that you want, that the user is going to like working with your program, and that everything is going to proceed as normal and do what you want. Take some time to practice these examples and see how they can work for you in order to handle any of the exceptions that come up in your code.

Chapter 9: Data Analysis with Python

Another topic that we need to explore a bit here is how Python, and some of the libraries that come with it, can work with the process of data analysis. This is an important process for any businesses because it allows them to take all of the data and information they have been collecting for a long time, and then can put it to good use once they understand what has been said within the information. It can be hard for a person to go through all of this information and figure out what is there, but for a data analyst who is able to use Python to complete the process, it is easy to find the information and the trends that you need.

The first thing that we need to look at here though is what data analysis is all about. Data analysis is going to be the process that companies can use in order to extract out useful, relevant, and even meaningful information from the data they collect, in a manner that is systematic. This ensures that they are able to get the full information out of everything and see some great results in the process. There are a number of reasons that a company would choose to work on their own data analysis, and this can include:

1. Parameter estimation, which helps them to infer some of the unknowns that they are dealing with.
2. Model development and prediction. This is going to be a lot of forecasting in the mix.
3. Feature extraction which means that we are going to identify some of the patterns that are there.
4. Hypothesis testing. This is going to allow us to verify the information and trends that we have found.
5. Fault detection. This is going to be the monitoring of the process that you are working on to make sure that there aren't any biases that happen in the information.

One thing that we need to make sure that we are watching out for is the idea of bias in the information that we have. If you go into the data analysis with the idea that something should turn out a certain way, or that you are going to manipulate the data so it fits the ideas that you have, there are going to be some problems. You can always change the data to say what you would like, but this doesn't mean that you are getting the true trends that come with this information, and you may be missing out on some of the things that you actually need to know about.

This is why a lot of data analysts will start this without any kind of hypothesis at all. This allows them to see the actual trends that come with this, and then see where the information is going to take you, without any kind of slant with the information that you have. This can make life easier and ensures that you are actually able to see what is truly in the information, rather than what you would like to see in that information.

Now, there are going to be a few different types of data that you can work with. First, there is going to be the deterministic. This is going to also be known as the data analysis that is non-random. And then there is going to be the stochastic, which is pretty much any kind that is not going to fit into the category of deterministic.

The Data Life Cycle

As we go through this information, it is important to understand some of the different phases that come with the data life cycle. Each of these comes together to ensure that we are able to understand the information that is presented to us and that we are able to use all of the data in the most efficient and best way possible.

There are a few stages that are going to come with this data life cycle, and we are going to start out with some of the basics to discuss each one to help us see what we are able to do with the data available to us. First, we work with data capture. The first experience that an individual or a company should have with a data item is to have it pass through the firewalls of the enterprise. This is going to be known as the Data Capture, which is basically going to be the act of creating values of data that do not exist yet and have never actually existed in that enterprise either. There are three ways that you can capture the data including:

1. Data acquisition: This is going to be the ingestion of data that is already existing that was produced by the organization but outside of the chosen enterprise.
2. Data entry: This is when we are dealing with the creation of new data values to help with the enterprise and it is done by devices or human operators that can help to generate the data needed.
3. Signal reception: This is where we are going to capture the data that a device has created with us, typically in the control system, but can be found in the Internet of Things if we would like.

The next part is going to be known as Data Maintenance. This is going to be where you supply the data to points at which data synthesis and data usage can occur in the next few steps. And it is best if you are able to work out the points so that they are going to be ready to go in this kind of phase.

What we will see during the data maintenance is that we are working to process the data, without really working to derive any value out of it yet. This is going to include integration changed data, cleansing, and making sure that the data is in the right format and as complete as possible before we get started. This ensures that no matter what method or algorithm you choose to work with here, you are going to be able to have the data ready to go.

Once you have been able to maintain the data and get it all cleaned up, it is time to work on the part known as data synthesis. This is a newer phase in the cycle and there are some places where you may not see this happen. This is going to be where we create some of the values of data through inductive logic, and using some of the data that we have from somewhere else as the input. The data synthesis is going to be the arena of analytics that is going to use modeling of some kind to help you get the right results in the end.

Data usage comes next. This data usage is going to be the part of the process where we are going to apply the data as information to tasks that the enterprise needs to run and then handle the management on its own. This would be a task that normally falls outside of your life cycle for the data. However, data is becoming such a central part of the model for most businesses and having this part done can make a big difference.

For example, the data itself can be a service or a product, or at least part of this service or product. This would then make it a part of the data usage as well. The usage of the data is going to have some special challenges when it comes to data governance. One of these is whether it is legal to use the data in the ways that most people in business would like. There could be some issues like contractual or regulatory constraints on how we can use this data and it is important that these are maintained as much as possible.

Once we have figured out the data usage, it is time to move on to data publication. In being used, it may be possible that our single data value may be sent outside of the enterprise. This is going to be known as the data publication, which we can define as the sending of data to a location that is not within the enterprise.

A good example of this would be when you have a brokerage that sends out some monthly statements to their client. Once the data has been sent outside the enterprise, it is de facto impossible to get that information back. When the values of data are wrong and you publish it, it is impossible to correct them because they are now beyond the reach of your enterprise. The idea of Data Governance, like we talked about before, is going to have to handle how this information that is incorrect can be handled with.

Next on the list is the data archival. We will see that the single data value that we are working with can sometimes experience a lot of different rounds of usage and then publication, but eventually, it is going to reach the very end of its life. The first part of this means that we need to be able to take the value of the data and archive it. When we work on the process of Data Archival, it is going to mean that we are copying the data to an environment where it is stored in case we need it again, in an active production environment, and then we will remove the data from all of those active environments as well.

This kind of archive for the data is simply going to be a place where the data is stored, but where no publication, usage, or maintenance is going to happen. If necessary, it is possible to take any of the data that is in the archive and bring it back out to use again.

And finally, we reach the part of data purging. This is going to be the end that comes with our single data value and the life cycle that it has gone through. Data purging is going to be when we remove every copy of data from the enterprise. If possible, you will reach this information through the archive. If there is a challenge from Data Governance at this point, it is just there to prove that the information and the data have gone through the proper purging procedure at that time.

Working with data analysis and why it is important

With this in mind, we need to pay attention to why we would want to work on data analysis to start with? Do we really need to be able to look through all of this information to find the trends, or is there another method? Let's look at an example of what can happen when we do this data analysis and why you would want to use it.

Let's consider that we are looking at a set of data that includes information about the weather that occurred across the globe between the years 2015 to 2018. We are also going to have information that is base don the country between these years as well. So, there is going to be a percentage of ran within that country and we are going to have some data that concerns this in our set of data as well.

Now, what if you would like to go through all of that data, but you would like to only take a look at the data that comes with one specific country. Let's say that you would like to look at America and you want to see what percentage of rain it received between 2016 and 2017. Now, how are you going to get this information in a quick and efficient manner?

What we would need to do to make sure that we were able to get ahold of this particular set of data is to work with the data analysis. There are several algorithms, especially those that come from machine learning, that would help you to figure out the percentage of rain that America gets between 2016 to 2017. And this whole process is going to be known as what data analysis is really all about.

The Python Panda Library

When it comes to doing some data analysis in Python, the best extension that you can use is Pandas. This is an open-sourced library that works well with Python and it is going to provide you with a high level of performance, data structures that are easy for even a beginner to use, and tools to make data analysis easy with Python. There are a lot of things to enjoy about this language, and if you want to be able to sort through all of the great information that you have available with the help of Python, then this is the library that you need to work with.

There are a lot of things that you can enjoy when it comes to working on the Python library. First off, this is one of the most popular and easy to use libraries when it comes to data science and it is going to work on top of the NumPy library. The name of Pandas that was given to this library is derived from the word of Panel Data, which is going to be an Econometrics from Multidimensional data. And one thing that a lot of coders are going to like about working with Pandas is that it is able to take a lot of the data that you need, including a SQL database or a TSV and CSV file, and will use it to create an object in Python. This object is going to have columns as well as rows called the data frame, something that looks very similar to what we see with a table in statistical software including Excel.

There are many different features that are going to set Pandas apart from some of the other libraries that are out there. Some of the benefits that you are going to enjoy the most will include:

1. There are some data frames or data structures that are going to be high level compared to some of the others that you can use.
2. There is going to be a streamlined process in place to handle the tabular data, and then there is also a functionality that is rich for the time series that you want to work with.

3. There is going to be the benefit of data alignment, missing data-friendly statistics, merge, join, and groupby methods to help you handle the data that you have.
4. You are able to use the variety of structures for data in Pandas, and you will be able to freely draw on the functions that are present in SciPy and NumPy to help make sure manipulation and other work can be done the way that you want.

Before we move on from here, we also need to have a good look at what some of the types of data are when it comes to Pandas. Pandas is going to be well suited when it comes to a large amount of data and will be able to help you sort through almost any kind of data that you would like. Some of the data types that are going to be the most suitable for working with the Pandas library with Python will include:

1. Any kind of tabular data that is going to have columns that are heterogeneously typed.
2. Arbitrary matrix data that has labels for the columns and rows.
3. Unordered and ordered time-series data
4. Any other kinds of sets of data that are statistical and observational.

Working with the Pandas library is one of the best ways to handle some of the Python codings that you want to do with the help of data analysis. As a company, it is so important to be able to go through and not just collect data, but also to be able to read through that information and learn some of the trends and the information that is available there. being able to do this can provide your company with some of the insights that it needs to do better, and really grow while providing customer service.

There are a lot of different methods that you can use when it comes to performing data analysis. And some of them are going to work in a different way than we may see with Python or with the Pandas library. But when it comes to efficiently and quickly working through a lot of data, and having a multitude of algorithms and more that can sort through all of this information, working with the Python Pandas is the best option.

Chapter 10: Can I Test my Code?

As you are working on some of the codings that you would like to in Python, it is important that you stop on occasion and think about some of the steps that you can do to test out your code in Python. This is going to make sure that any code you have written out in Python is going to work the way that you want, and that there will not be any bugs that show up in the coding as well. We are going to spend some time in this chapter looking at how you can test out any codes that you are writing in Python, and how you can use this to your advantage to make your code strong and to make sure that it works properly.

Manual and Automated Testing

The good thing to consider here is that it is likely you have gone through and created a test without realizing it. Remember when you went through and ran your application and then made sure to use it for the first time? Did you stop here and test out the features and see if they were all working? This is known as a form of exploratory testing, and it is going to be considered a form of manual testing that you can use.

Exploratory testing is going to be a great way to learn more about a program and how it works. It is basically a type of testing that is going to be done without having a good solid plan in place. In this kind of test, you are not looking to get anything out of it or looking to see something specific happen. But you are just taking some time to open up your chosen application and poke around to see how things work.

To have a complete set of the manual tests, you have to make a list of all the different features that are available in the application, the different inputs that it is able to accept, and the results that you are expecting. Now, every time that you go through and try to make some changes to your code, it is time for you to go through every single item that is on that list, and double-check that it is working and doing what you want. Of course, this doesn't sound like a lot of fun and can make coding even more complicated for a beginner, which is why you may not use manual testing that much.

This is the place where we need to start talking more about automated testing. This kind of testing is going to be the execution of your test plan, which is the parts of the application that you wish to get tested, the order you want them tested in, and the expected responses you plan to get out of them, by a script rather than you or another programmer having to go through and do the work. Python is already going to provide us with some tools, as well as some libraries, to create the automated tests for your applications.

Integration Tests and Unit Tests

When we enter into the world of testing, there is going to be a lot of terminologies that happens around us. And now that you know a bit about manual testing and automated testing, and how they are different, it is time to take ourselves a bit deeper. Think about how you would go through and test the lights that are on your car. It is likely that you would turn on the lights, which is your test step, and either ask a friend to check or you would check on your own, whether the lights did turn on, and this is going to be the test assertion. Testing more than one component is going to be known as integration testing.

Think about all of the different parts that have to come together and work in the correct manner in order to make sure that even the simple task above is going to give you the results that you want. These components are going to be similar to what we see with all the parts that are in your application, all of the modules, functions, and classes that you have already been able to write.

One of the biggest challenges that you are going to face when doing an integration test is when it doesn't provide you with the results that you need. It is hard to go through and provide a diagnosis to an issue without being able to go through and isolate out which part of the system is doing the failing. If the lights don't turn on, think about how many problems could be present that are causing that one issue. Maybe the bulb is broken, the computer of the car is failing, the alternator isn't working, or the battery could be dead.

Now, if you have a newer car that has a good computer in it, it is going to tell you when the light bulbs have gone out, saving you some time and hassle. It is going to do this with the help of a unit test. The unit test is going to be a smaller test, one that is going to be able to check that a single component operates in the way that you want. A unit test is going to help you to go through all of the problems and isolate what is broken inside that application, setting it to the side to fix later.

There are going to be two types of tests that fit in with this. The first one is going to be known as the integration test that will check the components of your application to see if they operate with each other. And then there is the unit test that is going to spend some time checking out the small components that come with your application. It is possible for you to write out both the unit tests and the integration tests with the help of Python.

One of the first things that you will need to do when running one of these tests in your code is to choose which test runner is the best for you. There are a lot of different test runners out there for you to choose from with Python. The one that is already found in the standard library for Python is going to be the unittest. We are going to use this in order to help us get the work done in the next few pages. The principles that come with this one are going to be portable with ease to other frameworks. The three most popular test runners are going to include some of the following:

1. Pytest
2. Nose or nose2
3. Unittest

Choosing the test runner that is going to be the right one for you is going to look at the things that you want to get done during the test, along with some of your level of experience in the process. But first, we are going to explore a bit more about the unittest and how it can work for you.

Unittest is something that has been around with Python for some time. in fact, it was built into the standard library that comes with Python back during Python 2.1 and has been a standard of that every sense. You will most likely see this in some of the commercial applications of Python, along with some of the projects that are open-sourced. Unittest is going to contain both a testing framework that you can use and a test runner. It also has some requirements that are important and that we need to follow when it comes to executing and writing the tests. These strict and important requirements for your tests with unittest are going to include:

1. You need to make sure that your tests are put into classes as a method.
2. You can use a series of assertion methods that are special in the unittest. TestCase class is sometimes one that is used rather than the built-in assert statement.

Then we need to make sure that we are using all of this in the proper manner as well. To make sure that we are able to convert an example that you may have already worked on, or worked on earlier, to the test case with unittest, you would need to use the following steps to get it done:

1. Import, from your standard library the unittest.

2. Create a new class that we are going to call TestSum. This is the one that will inherit everything from the TestCase class.
3. You can then move on to converting the test functions over into methods by adding self as the argument that is used first.
4. Then we can move on to changing up some of the assertions. We want to change this to self.assertEqual() inside the class known as TestCase.
5. And the final step that we need to work on is changing the entry point on the command line so that it calls up the unittest.main().

Now that we know a few of the instructions that we need to follow in order to run one of our own tests, it is time to look at some of the steps and the code that is needed to create a new file test_sum_Unittest.py. The code that we can use to make this happen includes:

import unittest

class TestSum(unittest.TestCase):

  def test_sum(self):

```
self.assertEqual(sum([1, 2, 3]), 6, "Should be 6")

def test_sum_tuple(self):
    self.assertEqual(sum((1, 2, 2)), 6, "Should be 6")

if __name__ == '__main__':
    unittest.main()
```

Before you try to write your own test though, we need to make sure that we know the right steps that are needed in order to structure one of these simple tests. Before you really try to dive into writing some of these tests, there are going to be a few decisions that you have to make. you need to first figure out what you would like to test. And then you need to figure out whether or not you are writing what is known as an integration test or a unit test. From here, you need to have the right kind of workflow in place to help get it all done. The loose schedule that you should follow with your workflow should include:

1. Create the inputs that you would like to use.
2. Execute the code that you are trying to test, making sure that you are able to capture the output that it gives.
3. Make sure that you compare the output against what result you were hoping to get. If there are differences, it is time to explore why.

For this application, we are going to take some time to test out the function of sum(). There are many different kinds of behaviors that we can look for in this kind of function to see if it is working in a proper manner. We could check out whether it can sum a list of whole numbers, also known as integers, if it is able to sum out a set or a tuple, if it is able to sum out a list of floats, what is going to happen with the code if you provide it with a value that is seen as bad and what is going to happen when you use this and one of the values ends up being negative?

The most simple out of all these tests are going to be the one that is able to list out the integers. We are going to start this one out by creating our own file that has test.py in it. We are going to use the code below to help us get this done:

import unittest

from my_sum import sum

class TestSum(unittest.TestCase):
  def test_list_int(self):
    """

    Test that it can sum a list of integers

```
"""
    data = [1, 2, 3]
    result = sum(data)
    self.assertEqual(result, 6)


if __name__ == '__main__':
    unittest.main()
```

There is a lot that goes on here in this code, and we are going to take a moment to look at it a bit closer. We see that it is going to be able to import the function of sum() from our package that we created earlier. Then it is going to define out a new test case class that we called TestSum, which is going to inherit the information from unittest.TestCase. It is also able to define the test method that we are using. In this one, we are working with test_list_int() in order to test out the different integers that we are working with. This allows us to declare a value that has data with a list of numbers, can help to assign the results of the my_sum.sum(data) to a result variable then it can assert that the value of result equals 6 by using the .assertEqual() method on your class.

Now, the last step that we need to use in order to write out a test is to make sure that we can validate the output we get against a known response. This is going to be the process of an assertion.

There are going to be a few best practices that you are able to follow when it comes to writing your own assertions and these will include:

1. Make sure that any test you try to run is repeatable and then run the test more than one time in order to ensure it is going to provide you with the same kind of result and answer each time.
2. Try and assert results that are going to relate to the input data that you have, such as checking that the result is actually going to be the sum of values in the sum() example.

Before we end this chapter, we need to take some time to look at a few of the side effects that come with writing our own tests. It is not always going to be as simple as it seems or as simple as looking back at some of the return value that comes with the function. Often, making sure that you can execute a piece of code is going to alter some of the other parts that happen in the environment, such as the attribute of a class, one of the files that are on the filesystem, or a value that should be in your database.

These issues are going to be known as the side effects, and they are definitely a big and important part when it comes to your testing. Deciding if the side effect is the part that is being tested or not before including it on your list of assertions can make a big difference in the kind of results that you would like to get, and whether they are going to turn out the way that you would like.

If you find that the unit of code that you are trying to test ends up with a ton of side effects, then it is possible that you are breaking the Single Responsibility Principle. This is basically going to mean that the part of the code that you are working on is already doing too much at once, and it is better for it to have everything refactored. Following this kind of principle is going to be one of the best ways that you can design out a code that is easy to write, repeatable, and simple to test for while still doing what you would like.

Testing is not always one of the best or most fun experiences when it comes to all of the codings that you can do. But it is definitely something that you need to add into the mix and that you need to focus on to ensure that your code is going to work in the manner that you want. When this is organized and ready to work, and you have been able to try out the testing at least a few times to make sure you get the right results, then you know your code is ready to use.

Chapter 11: Python and Artificial Intelligence

Artificial intelligence is something that is taking over the world. Many projects are now relying on this kind of programming to help make sure that things line up the way that they should, and that the program is able to perform and think on its own. It is amazing what artificial intelligence is able to do, taking on more things than we would have been able to do in the past.

The first thing that we need to explore is the idea of artificial intelligence. We already spent some time on Python and some of the different things that you are able to do with the programming of this, so knowing how to add in some of this coding to artificial intelligence, and knowing more about what AI consists of can make a big difference.

First, artificial intelligence is going to be one of the many sub-fields that fit in with computer science. It has a goal of enabling the development of computers so that these machines are able to do the tasks that are often reserved for people. This could happen in particular things that involve a person acting in an intelligent manner. This was a term that a researcher from Stanford, John McCarthy, coined in 1956 during what is known today as The Dartmouth Conference and the core mission that comes with artificial intelligence was then defined.

If we are able to start out or exploration with this definition then it is reasonable to think that any kind of program is considered AI if it does something that we would normally think of as intelligent in humans. The way that the program goes about doing this is not going to be the biggest issue. Just that the program is actually able to do this work. That is, it is AI if it is smart, but it doesn't have to necessarily be smart like us.

It turns out that each programmer is going to have their own goals when it comes to working on systems built on AI, and these are all going to really fall within three camps, based on how close the machines are building line up with how people behave and think.

For some, the whole goal of using AI is to build up a system that is able to think in the exact same manner that humans do, but usually in a faster and more efficient way. and then there are those programmers who just want to get the job done and they are not going to care of the computation has anything to do with the thoughts that humans have. And finally, there are some people in between who are going to use human reasoning as a model that can inform and inspire but not as the final target for imitation.

The work that is aimed at getting the system set up to simulate human reasoning tends to be known as strong AI. This is because any of the results can be used in order to not only build systems that think but are also able to help us explain how humans think as well. However, it is still something that we have not seen on a regular basis because it is a really hard problem for us to solve. When that time does come, and we start to see more of this in technology and in our daily lives, then it is going to be a big day and will make a big difference in what we are able to see in our lives.

Then the work that is able to fall into the second camp, the one that is aimed at just being able to get the system to work is going to be known as the weak AI. This means that while we might be able to build up a system that kind of behaves like a human does the results is not going to tell us anything about how a person is going to think. One example of this in work is the Deep Blue from IBM, a system that was a master chess player, but it was not able to play in a similar manner to humans.

And then there is the camp that is in between the strong and the weak AI and we are going to call this third came the in-between.

These are the systems that are going to be inspired and otherwise informed by human reasoning. This tends to be where most of the more powerful work in AI and other forms of computer science is going on today. These systems are going to use the reasoning of humans as a guide, but they do not have the end goal to perfectly model it.

A good example of what falls into this third category is IBM Watson. This program builds up evidence for the answers that it is able to find simply by looking at thousands of different texts so that it gains a good amount of confidence in the conclusion that it has. It is going to combine the ability to recognize a pattern in the texts that it reads with the ability to weigh the evidence that matching those patterns provides.

The development that came with this kind of program was guided by the observations of how people are able to come to various conclusions without us having a set of rules that we have to follow, and instead it is going to build up a collection of evidence that helps to back it up. Just like how humans are able to do, Watson is going to be able to get to notice some of the patterns that are found in the text that provides a bit of evidence and then will add up all of the different parts that it has in order to get that answer.

In addition, some of the deep learning that has come with Google is going to have a similar kind of feel. We mean that it is going to be inspired by the structure that we actually see in the brain. Informed by the behavior of the neurons, the systems of deep learning are going to function by learning layers of representations for tasks including speech recognition and image recognition. This may not be exactly the same as the brain is going to do the work, but this is something that does inspire it a bit.

The thing that we need to remember and take away here is that in order to look at a system and consider it a part of AI, rather than just a really good program, is that it doesn't have to just work the way that we do exactly. It just needs to be a program that is smart and can do some of the things that we talked about in this chapter.

Another thing that we need to take a look at while we are on this target is the difference between general AI and narrow AI. There is the narrow AI system that is going to be designed to handle a specific task, and then there are the general AI that is meant to have the ability to reason on things in general. Sometimes, it is easy to get a bit confused by this distinction, and this can make us mistakenly interpret specific results in a specific area as somehow being able to scope across all of the intelligent behavior.

Systems that are able to recommend things to you based on what you have done on that site in the past are going to be different compared to the systems that are going to take a look at an image and recognize that. And both of these are going to be different from any kind of system that is able to make decisions based on the syntheses of evidence. These are all going to be examples of narrow AI in practice, but you do not want to generalize them to address all of the issues that can happen with an intelligent machine that is able to work on its own. They are all smart and can all work with artificial intelligence, but they all do different things.

Now that we know a bit more about what artificial intelligence is all about, it is time to take a look at why you would like to work with artificial intelligence and the Python language altogether. These are used to help you write some of the programs that you want and can make a complicated task like artificial intelligence and make it as easy as possible.

There are a number of different benefits that are going to come with using Python as part of your plan with artificial intelligence. Whether you are a startup or a bigger company, you will find that Python is going to be able to provide a huge list of benefits to all. Using this language is such that it should not be limited to just one activity and it is growing popularity has allowed it to enter into things like natural language processing, artificial intelligence, data science, and machine learning.

But then this brings us some questions as well. How is Python is able to gain such momentum in AI and why would we want to work with this kind of language to help us to really work on some of this part of computer science, rather than using another kind of coding language to get this done. There are a lot of benefits to using Python to help you to work with machine learning and artificial intelligence, and some of these benefits include:

You can use less code. AI is going to involve a ton of code and a lot of algorithms to help make up that code. This is how you get the program to learn and act in the manner that you would like. You will find that adding Python into the mix can help to ease some of the testings, and even keep the lines of code needed for each algorithm down to a minimum. Python is going to be able to make the writing as well as the execution of the codes as simple as possible, it is able to implement the same logic with as much as 1/5th of the code compared to many of the other coding languages that you want to use. And because of the interpreted approach that comes with it, you will be able to get some of the artificial intelligence work that you want to be done without having to write out as much confusing code to get it done.

The next benefit that comes with using the Python language when you want to work on artificial intelligence is all of the prebuilt libraries. Python is going to have a ton of different libraries that are going to help you with all of the projects that you want to do in AI. There are a few different ones that you can work with including Scikit-Learn, SciPy, NumPy and more. Python implementation of algorithms are going to be some of the best, and you are going to be able to pull them out of a lot of the libraries that you can find available through Python already. Having these dedicated libraries is going to save you a lot of time compared to coding on items that are still at the base level.

And then we can move on to the support that you will receive with this kind of coding, even when you are working on AI. Python is an open-sourced program that has an amazing community present. There is a ton of resources that are available which will ensure that any developer is up to speed on what they need to know in no time. there is also a big community of active coders who are willing to answer questions and help programmers no matter which stage they may be in when it comes to the cycle of developing.

The platform agnostics is important. Python is going to provide us with the flexibility to provide an API from an existing language which is going to make sure that we are able to get the work done. If it is also a platform-independent that is going to help us to get things done. With just a few changes in codes, you are going to get your app up and running in a new operating system. This is going to save the developers a lot of time when it comes to testing on all of the different platforms and migrating code the way that you would like. This makes it easier to use the AI that you are developing with Python on more than one platform, even if you are not going through and testing each of them.

Of course, Python is going to provide us with a good deal of flexibility, no matter what kind of code that we are working on. Flexibility is going to be a big advantage that comes with working on the Python code. With the option to choose between the scripting and the approach that is used with this language, Python is going to be so great no matter which program you are working with. It is also going to work as a good backend and it is suitable for helping out with almost any kind of data structure and linking them all together in the process. The option to check a majority of the code in the IDE on its own is going to be another big plus for developers who are struggling with some of the algorithms that come with this kind of program

And the final benefit of working with the Python language with artificial intelligence is that it is really popular. Right now, Python is already being able to win the heart of many new programmers who are coming into the market and trying to make their mark with their own codes. Though AI projects need a very experienced programmer to get them done, it is possible to use Python in order to smoothen up some of the learning curves. It is so much easier for us to look for developers in Python than it is for programmers in different languages, especially in some different parts of the world depending on where you are looking.

There is just so much to love about using the Python language, and this has taken the world by storm, helping us find a lot of different programs and programmers that use Python. Add in the active community and some of the extended libraries along with some of the ever-developing and improving code, and you can see why Python has turned into one of the most used languages in coding to work with today.

It is possible that some of the projects that you are going to work with over time can get a bit tricky. This is where using Python and some of the libraries that come with this are going to become handy and can be a good thing. In our last chapter, we are going to explore not only some exercises that you are able to do with Python in particular, but also some that you can do with machine learning and artificial intelligence to help you really explore what is available and see just how much easier the Python language can make some of the more complicated coding tasks.

Chapter 12: Python and Machine Learning

The final topic that we need to spend some time on is the idea of machine learning and how Python is going to be able to work along with this idea. Machine learning is going to be a type of artificial intelligence that is going to help us to really work on some of the different types of learning that a system is able to do. This one goes a bit more specifically into this kind of learning than we are going to see with artificial intelligence, and Python, along with a lot of the libraries that come with it, can help us to get the work done as easily as possible in your coding.

This kind of learning process is going to be helpful when it is time to start with observations, also known as data, like instructions, direct experience, surveys, examples, and more in order to figure out what trends and patterns are found in the data. Then the predictions that are pulled out of this data are used to help us know what is going to happen in the future. One of the main goals that is going to happen when we work with machine learning is that it will ensure that the computer is going to learn in a manner that is more automatic, meaning that it is able to learn how to do things without the help of a person or any programming coming in and making the adjustments here.

When you work with machine learning, you will find that it makes analyzing large quantities of data easier than ever. Machine learning can give us some results that are profitable, but of course, you first have to learn how to set it up, and there are a few resources that are needed before you are able to make this all happen. This type of coding is often going to take a bit more time to work with because you are basically training the models of machine learning to do what you want, even when you aren't there, which can really increase how much the system can do.

There are a lot of different things that you are able to use machine learning. Any time that you aren't sure how the end result is going to turn up, or you aren't sure what the input of the other person could be, you will find that machine learning can help you get through some of these problems. If you want the computer to be able to go through a long list of options and find patterns or find the right result, then machine learning is going to work the best for you. Some of the other things that machine learning can help out with include:

1. Being able to recognize the voice of someone
2. Being able to recognize the facial features of someone

3. The use of a search engine. You will find that the program here is going to be able to learn based on the answers that the user has put in, or the queries that they are searching for. Over time, the search engine will know more about what the user is looking for and can learn how to provide the best results over time.

4. As you are shopping, you may notice that there are recommendations that show up on the system as you go. These recommendation channels are an example of machine learning.

5. Doing the data analysis that we talked about earlier. The machine learning process is going be able to sort through a lot of data about customers and finances and can make some good predictions about what a company should consider doing in order to increase how many happy customers and profits they can make along the way.

Of course, these are just a few of the more well-known examples that are out there when it comes to machine learning and trying to get the computer to figure out the right course of action to take on its own. Many of the programs that you are going to learn how to code with, including some of the ones that are in this guidebook, are going to be a bit easier to handle than this. They are going to be there, telling the computer exactly how it should behave and what it is going to do in each situation. But when it comes to working on machine learning and other parts of artificial intelligence, this is not going to be enough to see results.

When we go through some of the traditional codings that we have talked about in this guidebook, you will need to figure out, or at least try as much as you can, to limit how many choices your user is going to get to use. And then you would add in the catch-all to the program in order to make sure you didn't miss something. This works well for a lot of the programs that you want to write, but you can imagine that this is going to be falling short in some areas based on what you want to accomplish.

With machine learning, we need to work with a program that is able to adapt and change. We need to have a type of coding that is going to look at a problem and then figure out how it can learn from it and do what the user wants, in ways that traditional programming can't do. And this is where Python is going to be able to get into the mix and help us get the work done.

But first, we need to explore that there are three main types of machine learning algorithms that can be used. Each of these is going to work in a slightly different manner, but they can all be useful based on the kind of program that you want to write out and what needs to happen in the end. The three types of machine learning that you can work with include supervised machine learning, reinforcement machine learning, and unsupervised machine learning.

First, we will look at the supervised machine learning. This is when the programmer is going to feed in a lot of different examples to the code, in the hopes that when the algorithm works properly, the code is going to have a good idea of the rules and how to follow them. Taking the examples that it learned, the program will be able to make accurate predictions and function as it should. It is possible that there will still be some mistakes in the process, but it will learn how to do better with more examples over time, and you will find that it becomes pretty accurate pretty quickly.

Then we can move on to the unsupervised machine learning. This is going to be where the program is just going to learn on its own, based on the actions of the user and without needing all of the examples that the other type of learning is going to provide. This is something that we see with voice recognition. There is no way that the programmer would be able to go in and give enough examples to handle this. Instead, the program just learns how to recognize different words, and the dialects and the different speech patterns and then it gets better at this over time.

And finally, we reach the reinforcement machine learning. This one is similar to what we are going to see with the unsupervised machine learning, but it is going to rely more on the idea of true and false. The more that the program is able to get true, the stronger it can become. But when it makes mistakes, it can remember that as well and will look for a better path the next time around.

From here, we need to take a look at the Python language and how it is going to work inside the codes that you want to write as well. There are other languages that are going to work pretty well when you do machine learning, but none offer as many libraries, the power, the speed, and even the ease of use as you are going to get when you decide to add in some Python coding to any machine learning project that you would like to do.

While we will take a look at Python and how it works in a bit, it is important to note that Python is one of the best languages to work with when it comes to machine learning. Python is a simple language, one that is easy enough for beginners to the world of programming to work with. Yet it still has enough power behind it to make sure that you can still get some of the intense codes done that you would like. The language has a large library, works well with other coding languages if you decide to implement them together, and it is easy enough to read, even if you don't have any kind of coding practice or experience in the past.

Many of the codes and the different parts of the coding language that we discussed in this guidebook are going to be helpful even when you work with machine learning and some of the more complicated tasks that we will need to handle with machine learning. We will look in the next chapter at one of the machine learning algorithms that you are able to do with Python and you will see that while the code may be a bit longer than some of the others we have discussed, it is still pretty simple to work with and will include a lot of the parts you are already familiar with.

There is just so much that you are going to be able to do when it comes to working with machine learning, and when it is combined with the Python coding language, as well as with artificial intelligence and data analysis like we talked about through this guidebook, you will find that there is just so much that you can do, even with the beginner programming that we discussed in this guidebook!

Chapter 13: Practical Codes and Exercises to Use Python

Now that we have had some time to learn how to work with the Python code, it is time to take a look at some practical examples of working with this kind of coding language. We will do a few different Python exercises here so that you can have a little bit of fun, and get a better idea of how you would use the different topics that we have talked about in this guidebook to your benefit. There are a lot of neat programs that you are able to use when you write in Python, but the ones in this chapter will give you a good idea of how to write codes, and how to use the examples that we talked about in this guidebook in real coding. So let's get started!

Creating a Magic 8 Ball

The first project that we are going to take a look at here is how to create your own Magic 8 ball. This will work just like a regular magic 8 ball, but it will be on the computer. You can choose how many answers that you would like to have available to those who are using the program but we are going to focus on having eight responses show up for the user at a random order so they get something different each time.

Setting up this code is easier than you think. Take some time to study this code, and then write it out into the compiler. See how many of the different topics we discussed in this guidebook show up in this code as well. The code that you need to use in order to create a program that includes your own Magic 8 ball will include:

```
# Import the modules
import sys
import random


ans = True


while ans:
        question = raw_input("Ask the magic 8 ball a question:
(press enter to quit)")


answers = random.randint(1,8)


if question == ""
        sys.exit()


elif answers ==1:
        print("It is certain")
```

```python
elif answers == 2:
    print("Outlook good")

elif answers == 3:
print("You may rely on it")

elif answers == 4:
    print("Ask again later")

elif answers == 5:
    print("Concentrate and ask again")

elif answers == 6:
    print("Reply hazy, try again.")

elif answers == 7:
    print("My reply is no")

elif answers == 8:
    print("My sources say no")
```

Remember in this program, we chose to go with eight options because it is a Magic 8 ball and that makes the most sense. But if you would like to add in some more options, or work on another program that is similar and has more options, then you would just need to keep adding in more of the elif statement to get it done. This is still a good example of how to use the elif statement that we talked about earlier and can give us some good practice on how to use it. You can also experiment a bit with the program to see how well it works and make any changes that you think are necessary to help you get the best results.

How to make a Hangman Game

The next project that we are going to take a look at is creating your own Hangman game. This is a great game to create because it has a lot of the different options that we have talked about throughout this guidebook and can be a great way to get some practice on the various topics that we have looked at. We are going to see things like a loop present, some comments, and more and this is a good way to work with some of the conditional statements that show up as well.

Now, you may be looking at this topic and thinking it is going to be really hard to work with a Hangman game. It is going to have a lot of parts that go together as the person makes a guess and the program tries to figure out what is going on, whether the guesses are right, and how many chances the user gets to make these guesses. But using a lot of the different parts that we have already talked about in this guidebook can help us to write out this code without any problems. The code that you need to use in order to create your very own Hangman game in Python includes:

```
# importing the time module
importing time

#welcoming the user
Name = raw_input("What is your name?")

print("Hello, + name, "Time to play hangman!")

print("
"

#wait for 1 second
time.sleep(1)

print("Start guessing...")
time.sleep(.05)

#here we set the secret
word = "secret"
```

```
#creates a variable with an empty value
guesses = ' '

#determine the number of turns
turns = 10

#create a while loop

#check if the turns are more than zero
while turns > 0:

        #make a counter that starts with zero
        failed = 0

        #for every character in secret_word
        for car in word:
        #see if the character is in the players guess
        if char in guesses:

        #print then out the character
        print char,

        else
```

```
# if not found, print a dash
print "_",

# and increase the failed counter with one
failed += 1

#if failed is equal to zero

#print You Won
if failed == 0:
print("You Won")

#exit the script
        Break

print

# ask the user go guess a character
guess = raw_input("guess a character:")

#set the players guess to guesses
guesses += guess

# if the guess is not found in the secret word
if guess not in word:
```

```
#turns counter decreases with 1 (now 9)
turns -= 1


#print wrong
        print("Wrong")


# how many turns are left
        Print("You have," + turns, 'more guesses')


#if the turns are equal to zero
        if turns == 0


#print "You Loose"
```

Okay, so yes, this is a longer piece of code, especially when it is compared to the Magic 8 Ball that we did above, but take a deep breath, and go through it all to see what you recognize is there. This isn't as bad as it looks, and much of it is actually comments to help us see what is going on at some of the different parts of the code. This makes it easier to use for our own needs and can ensure that we know what is going on in the different parts. There are probably a lot of other things that show up in this code that you can look over and recognize that we talked about earlier as well. This makes it easier for you to get the code done!

Making your own K-means algorithm

Now that we have had some time to look at a few fun games and examples that you are able to do with the help of the Python code, let's take a moment to look at some of the things that you can do with machine learning and artificial intelligence with your coding. We spent some time talking about how you can work with these and some of the different parts of the code, as well as how Python is going to work with the idea of machine learning. And now we are going to take that information and create one of our own machine learning algorithms to work with as well.

Before we work on a code for this one, we need to take a look at what this k-means clustering means. This is a basic algorithm that works well with machine learning and is going to help you to gather up all of the data that you have in your system, the data that isn't labeled at the time, and then puts them all together in their own little group of a cluster.

The idea of working with this kind of cluster is that the objects that fall within the same cluster, whether there are just two or more, are going to be related to each other in some manner or another, and they are not going to be that similar to the data points that fall into the other clusters. The similarity here is going to be the metric that you will want to use in order to show us the strength that is in the relationship between the two.

When you work on this particular algorithm, it is going to be able to form some of the clusters that you need of the data, based on how similar the values of data that you have. You will need to go through and give them a specific value for K, which will be how many clusters that you would like to use. It is best to have at least two, but the number of these clusters that you work with will depend on how much data you have and how many will fit in with the type of data that you are working with.

With this information in mind and a good background of what the K-means algorithm is going to be used for, it is time to explore a bit more about how to write your own codes and do an example that works with K-means. This helps us to practice a bit with machine learning and gives us a chance to practice some of our own new Python skills.

```
import numpy as np
import matplotlib.pyplot as plt


def d(u, v):
```

```
diff = u - v
return diff.dot(diff)


def cost(X, R, M):
  cost = 0
  for k in xrange(len(M)):
    for n in xrange(len(X)):
      cost += R[n,k]*d(M[k], X[n])
  return cost
```

After this part, we are going to take the time to define your function so that it is able to run the k-means algorithm before plotting the result. This is going to end up with a scatterplot where the color will represent how much of the membership is inside of a particular cluster. We would do that with the following code.

```
def plot_k_means(X, K, max_iter=20, beta=1.0):
  N, D = X.shape
  M = np.zeros((K, D))
  R = np.ones((N, K)) / K
```

```python
# initialize M to random
for k in xrange(K):
    M[k] = X[np.random.choice(N)]

grid_width = 5
grid_height = max_iter / grid_width
random_colors = np.random.random((K, 3))
plt.figure()

costs = np.zeros(max_iter)
for i in xrange(max_iter):
    # moved the plot inside the for loop
    colors = R.dot(random_colors)
    plt.subplot(grid_width, grid_height, i+1)
    plt.scatter(X[:,0], X[:,1], c=colors)

    # step 1: determine assignments / responsibilities
    # is this inefficient?
    for k in xrange(K):
        for n in xrange(N):
            R[n,k] = np.exp(-beta*d(M[k], X[n])) / np.sum(
np.exp(-beta*d(M[j], X[n])) for j in xrange(K) )

    # step 2: recalculate means
    for k in xrange(K):
```

$M[k] = R[:,k].dot(X) / R[:,k].sum()$

$costs[i] = cost(X, R, M)$
if $i > 0$:
   if $np.abs(costs[i] - costs[i-1]) < 10e-5$:
      break

plt.show()

Notice here that both the M and the R are going to be matrices. The R is going to become the matrix because it holds onto 2 indices, the k and the n. M is also a matrix because it is going to contain the K individual D-dimensional vectors. The beta variable is going to control how fuzzy or spread out the cluster memberships are and will be known as the hyperparameter. From here, we are going to create a main function that will create random clusters and then call up the functions that we have already defined above.

def main():
   # assume 3 means
   D = 2 # so we can visualize it more easily
   s = 4 # separation so we can control how far apart the means are

```python
mu1 = np.array([0, 0])
mu2 = np.array([s, s])
mu3 = np.array([0, s])

N = 900 # number of samples
X = np.zeros((N, D))
X[:300, :] = np.random.randn(300, D) + mu1
X[300:600, :] = np.random.randn(300, D) + mu2
X[600:, :] = np.random.randn(300, D) + mu3

# what does it look like without clustering?
plt.scatter(X[:,0], X[:,1])
plt.show()

K = 3 # luckily, we already know this
plot_k_means(X, K)

# K = 5 # what happens if we choose a "bad" K?
# plot_k_means(X, K, max_iter=30)

# K = 5 # what happens if we change beta?
# plot_k_means(X, K, max_iter=30, beta=0.3)


if __name__ == '__main__':
```

main()

Yes, this process is going to take some time to write out here, and it is not always an easy process when it comes to working through the different parts that come with machine learning and how it can affect your code. But when you are done, you will be able to import some of the data that your company has been collecting, and then determine how this compares using the K-means algorithm as well.

Conclusion

Thank for making it through to the end of Python *for Beginners*. Let's hope it was informative and able to provide you with all of the tools you need to achieve your goals whatever they may be.

The next step is to take some time to look at the different examples that we have explored in this guidebook and use these to help you learn more about how to work with the Python language, and some of the neat things that you are able to do with this coding language. There are a lot of other coding languages out there that you are able to work with, but Python is one of the best that works for most beginner programmers, providing the power and the ease of use that you are looking for when you first get started in this kind of coding language. This guidebook took the time to explore how Python works, along with some of the different types of coding that you can do with it.

In addition to seeing a lot of examples of how you can code in Python and how you can create some of your own programs in this language, we also spent some time looking at how to work with Python when it comes to the world of machine learning, artificial intelligence, and data analysis. These are topics and parts of technology that are taking off and many programmers are trying to learn more about. And with the help of this guidebook, you will be able to handle all of these, even as a beginner in Python.

When you are ready to learn more about how to work with the Python coding language and how you are able to make sure that you can even use Python along with data analysis, artificial intelligence, and machine learning, make sure to check out this guidebook to help you get started.

Finally, if you found this book useful in any way, a review on Amazon is always appreciated!